Celtic Mythology

A Collection of the Best Celtic Myths

Jason Dodd

Table Of Contents

Introduction

Welcome to "Celtic Mythology: A Collection of the Best Celtic Myths," a captivating journey into the heart of ancient Celtic lore. This book is a treasure trove of tales that have been woven into the fabric of history, culture, and the collective consciousness of the Celtic people. From the mist-shrouded hills of Ireland to the rugged coastlines of Scotland, from the sacred groves of Wales to the mystical lands of Brittany, Cornwall, and the Isle of Man, the Celtic world is replete with stories of heroism, adventure, magic, and mystery.

Our opening chapter serves as a gateway to the celestial realms, introducing the reader to the illustrious pantheon of Celtic deities. These gods and goddesses, each wielding their unique powers and embodying distinct realms of existence, offer a profound glimpse into the Celtic spiritual landscape. Through tales of creation, destruction, love, and betrayal, we explore the intricate narratives that paint these divine beings not just as distant, omnipotent figures, but as entities deeply intertwined with the fate of the world and its inhabitants.

Venturing forth into the second chapter, the narrative shifts from the divine to the legendary, focusing on iconic figures such as Cú Chulainn, Fionn Mac Cumhaill, and Oisín. These characters, though mortal, possess qualities that elevate them to a near-mythic status. Their stories, brimming with feats of strength, wisdom, and valor, serve not only as captivating tales of adventure but also as moral compasses, guiding the listener through the complex labyrinth of Celtic ethical and societal values.

The third chapter expands the horizon further, delving into the diverse branches of Celtic mythology, including Irish, Scottish, Welsh, Breton, Cornish, and Manx traditions. This exploration reveals the rich tapestry of cultural narratives that, while sharing common threads, exhibit a fascinating array of perspectives and themes unique to their regional origins. It is here that we begin to truly appreciate the depth and breadth of Celtic mythology, as a reflection of the natural and cultural landscapes from which it springs.

As we journey deeper into the heart of the book, each subsequent chapter unfolds a singular myth, meticulously chosen for its significance and beauty. From the haunting sorrow of "The Children of Lir" to the martial prowess and tragedy of "The Cattle Raid of Cooley"; from the wisdom-laden tale of "The Salmon of Knowledge" to the timeless love story of "Tristan and Iseult"; each narrative is a masterpiece, offering a window into the Celtic soul.

"Celtic Mythology: A Collection of the Best Celtic Myths" is more than just a compilation of stories; it is an odyssey that transports the reader across the thresholds of time and reality, into a realm where the ancient world's magic and mystique are alive and palpable. Through these pages, the legends of the Celts are not merely retold but rekindled, inviting you to partake in a legacy of wonder, bravery, and enchantment that has been passed down through the ages. Join us on this voyage, and let the ancient tales of the Celtic peoples awaken your imagination and stir your spirit.

CHAPTER 1:

The Celtic Pantheon

Celtic Mythology and its various component parts are host to a variety of different Gods and Goddesses, each with their own unique powers, roles, and lineage. In this chapter, you'll be introduced to these different deities and learn a little about each of them.

Irish Mythology

The Dagda

The Dagda is a prominent deity in Celtic mythology, particularly within the Irish tradition, where he is revered as a god of immense power and a pivotal figure among the Tuatha Dé Danann, the pantheon of pre-Christian gods in Ireland. His name, often interpreted to mean "the good god" or "the great god," reflects his multifaceted nature and the wide range of his dominion, encompassing aspects such as fertility, agriculture, magic, wisdom, and strength. The Dagda is depicted as a father figure, a protector, and a leader, wielding an array of magical items that underscore his vast abilities. Among these, his club, capable of both killing and restoring life, and his cauldron, from which no one goes away unsatisfied, are the most iconic. These items symbolize his power over life and death, as well as abundance and provision.

The Dagda's background in Celtic mythology is rich with tales that highlight his wisdom, his strategic prowess in battle, and his deep connections with the land and its cycles. He is often involved in stories that depict the Tuatha Dé Danann's struggles against their adversaries, such as the Fomorians, showcasing his role as a protector and a warrior. His relationships with other deities add layers to his character; for example, his liaisons with goddesses like the Morrígan, who embodies war and fate, further intertwine him with the themes of sovereignty and the protection of his people.

Lugh

Lugh is a prominent deity in Celtic mythology, renowned for his skills, versatility, and association with the sun and light. Known as Lugh Lamhfada, or "Lugh of the Long Arm," in Irish mythology, he is celebrated for his expertise in multiple crafts and arts, earning him the title of Samildánach or "master of all arts." His attributes include prowess as a warrior, magician, craftsman, and king, symbolizing the ideal of the accomplished and versatile hero.

Lugh's background is rich with adventure and significance. He is often described as a member of the Tuatha Dé Danann, the pantheon of gods in Irish mythology, and is a pivotal figure in their battles against the oppressive Fomorians, a group of malevolent beings who embody chaos and destruction. Lugh's most famous exploit is his leadership in the Battle of Mag Tuired, where his strategic genius and martial skills lead the Tuatha Dé Danann to a decisive victory, underscoring his role as a savior and protector of his people. This victory not only secured the freedom of the Tuatha Dé Danann from the Fomorian threat but also established Lugh's position as a king and a hero within the Celtic pantheon.

Lugh is also linked with the harvest festival of Lughnasadh, named in his honor, which celebrates the beginning of the harvest season. This festival, traditionally held on the 1st of August, underscores his connections to agriculture, prosperity, and the cyclical nature of life and the seasons.

The Morrígan

The Morrígan is a complex figure in Celtic mythology, often associated with war, fate, and sovereignty. She is sometimes presented as a singular deity and other times as a trio of sisters, which can include various combinations of goddesses such as Badb, Macha, and Nemain, among others. This trio is collectively known as the Morrígna. The Morrígan is often depicted as a crow or raven, creatures linked to war and death, symbolizing her role as a foreteller of doom and a manipulator of the fate of warriors on the battlefield.

Her background in the mythological narratives of the Celts is rich and multifaceted, intertwining her with the lives and destinies of other deities and heroes, such as Cú Chulainn, one of the most famous heroes of Irish mythology. In the tales of the Ulster Cycle, she is known to have both aided and challenged Cú Chulainn, showcasing her complex nature as both a protector and a challenger of heroes. The Morrígan's role extends beyond the battlefield; she is also a guardian of the land and its sovereignty, embodying the power and the tumultuous nature of the land itself.

Brigid

Brigid, in Celtic mythology, is a multifaceted goddess who embodies aspects of healing, poetry, smithcraft, and fertility, reflecting the Celts' reverence for the natural world and its cycles. She is often associated with fire, a symbol of the hearth and home, as well as inspiration, creativity, and the nurturing of life. Brigid is celebrated for her protective qualities, her patronage of craftspeople, healers, and poets, and her connection to the early spring, a time of renewal and rebirth.

Her background intertwines with the landscapes and cultural practices of the Celts, particularly in Ireland, where she is one of the most prominent deities. Brigid's role extends beyond the spiritual, as she is deeply integrated into the everyday lives of the Celtic people through festivals such as Imbolc, celebrated on February 1st. Imbolc marks the beginning of spring and is closely associated with Brigid, symbolizing new growth, the return of light, and the awakening of the land from its winter slumber.

Brigid's enduring presence in Celtic mythology and her transition into Christian tradition as Saint Brigid of Kildare, where she continues to be venerated, highlight her significance and the adaptability of her attributes across changing religious landscapes.

Aengus (Óengus)

Aengus, also known as Óengus, Óengus Óg, or Mac Óg, is a notable deity in Celtic mythology, particularly within the Irish tradition. He is often depicted as a god of love, youth, and poetic inspiration, embodying the ideal of eternal youth and beauty. Aengus is the son of the Dagda, one of the principal gods of the Tuatha Dé Danann, and Boann, a goddess associated with the River Boyne. His conception and birth are surrounded by tales of trickery and the manipulation of time, reflecting his association with enchantment and the supernatural.

Aengus is famed for his residence at Brú na Bóinne, an ancient Neolithic site in Ireland that is today known as Newgrange. One of his most famous mythological tales involves his search for a maiden he saw in a dream, who symbolizes love and beauty. After a lengthy quest, Aengus succeeds in finding and being united with this maiden, Caer, who is capable of transforming into a swan. This story, among others, highlights his role as a deity of love and the pursuit of desire.

In addition to his associations with love and youth, Aengus is also revered as a patron of young people and is believed to protect and guide them. His character is often invoked in tales and poetry for his ability to use his words and charms to navigate the challenges posed by the otherworldly aspects of Celtic mythology.

Danu (Anu/Ana)

Danu, also known as Anu or Ana, is a somewhat enigmatic figure in Celtic mythology, often considered a primordial mother goddess. While specific details about her myths and stories are less defined than those of other deities, Danu is widely recognized as a symbol of fertility, abundance, and the nurturing aspects of nature. She is believed to be the progenitor of the Tuatha Dé Danann, the tribe of gods and goddesses who are central to Irish mythology, which underscores her role as a mother figure and a source of life.

The lack of direct references and detailed stories about Danu in surviving Celtic myths may be due to the oral nature of these traditions and the subsequent influence of Christianization, which led to the loss or transformation of many earlier beliefs. Despite this, Danu's significance is inferred through the reverence her descendants, the

Tuatha Dé Danann, held for her. Her name is thought to be connected to rivers and water sources across Europe, such as the Danube, Dnieper, and Don rivers, highlighting her association with water, a vital element of fertility and life in ancient agrarian societies.

Manannán mac Lir

Manannán mac Lir is a prominent figure in Celtic mythology, particularly within Irish and Manx legends, where he is revered as a powerful sea deity and protector of the Otherworld, a realm of the dead and a place of eternal youth and beauty. His name, Manannán, is closely associated with the Isle of Man, suggesting a strong connection to this location in the Irish Sea. As "mac Lir," meaning "son of the sea," his identity as a god of the sea and maritime environments is further emphasized, showcasing his dominion over the oceans, weather, and navigation.

Manannán is often depicted as a benevolent and enigmatic figure, possessing a vast array of magical items that enhance his abilities to navigate between worlds, manipulate the weather, and shroud his movements in mist and mystery. Among his most famous possessions are his boat, the Scuabtuinne, which can navigate without sails; his horse, Aonbharr, which can travel over water as easily as land; and his invulnerable cloak of mists, which he uses to shield his movements and the entrance to the Otherworld.

In mythology, Manannán is known for his wisdom, his skill in diplomacy, and his role as a psychopomp, guiding souls to the Otherworld. He also plays a significant role in the tales of other deities and heroes, offering guidance, assistance, and occasionally challenges, to those who seek to navigate the complexities of the Celtic mythological landscape.

Boann

Boann is a goddess in Celtic mythology, closely associated with water and fertility. She is most famously linked to the River Boyne in Ireland, a river that bears her name (from the ancient Irish "Boand" or "Bóinn"). Boann's mythology is deeply intertwined with themes of wisdom, inspiration, and the transformative power of water, reflecting the Celts' reverence for natural elements and landscapes.

According to myth, Boann was the wife of Nechtan, a deity associated with a sacred well that contained immense wisdom and was surrounded by hazel trees, symbols of knowledge. The well, often described as the source of all rivers, was guarded and its waters were only accessible to Nechtan and his cup-bearers. Defying this prohibition, Boann approached the well, and her actions resulted in the waters rising up, either as a consequence of her challenge or as a deliberate act on her part to release the waters. This surge of water is said to have pursued Boann, eventually forming the River Boyne, and in some versions of the tale, it is suggested that this transformative event either imbued her with divine attributes or enhanced her existing goddess status.

Dian Cecht

Dian Cecht is a prominent figure in Celtic mythology, particularly within Irish legends, where he is revered as the god of healing and medicine. As a member of the Tuatha Dé Danann, the pantheon of pre-Christian Irish gods, Dian Cecht's skills as a healer and physician are legendary, embodying the ancient Celts' respect for the healing arts and the natural remedies of the earth.

According to mythology, Dian Cecht's most notable contributions include the creation of a miraculous well, the Well of Sláine, which possessed the power to heal the wounded and resurrect the dead. This well was particularly significant during the battles between the Tuatha Dé Danann and their adversaries, as it allowed the fallen warriors of the Tuatha Dé Danann to be healed or revived, ready to fight once again. This aspect of his mythology highlights the importance of healing and regeneration, themes central to the cyclical view of life and death in Celtic belief systems.

Dian Cecht's prowess was not limited to the mystical; he was also credited with remarkable feats of medical skill, such as fashioning a silver hand for his son Nuada, the king of the Tuatha Dé Danann, who had lost his arm in battle. This act of creating a functional prosthetic not only restored Nuada's physical form but also his kingship, as physical wholeness was a requisite for leadership among the Tuatha Dé Danann. Through these tales, Dian Cecht is portrayed as a figure whose knowledge and skills transcend the boundaries between the magical and the practical, showcasing the Celts' appreciation for the healing arts and the protectors and providers of health and wellness within their communities.

Goibniu

Goibniu is a significant figure in Celtic mythology, particularly within the Irish tradition, where he is revered as the god of blacksmithing, metalworking, and craftsmanship. As one of the Tuatha Dé Danann, the pantheon of pre-Christian Irish gods, Goibniu holds a crucial role in the mythological narratives, embodying the Celts' deep respect for the art of crafting and the transformative power of the forge.

Goibniu's most renowned attribute is his skill in forging weapons that were unerringly accurate and would always strike true. According to mythology, his craftsmanship was unparalleled, and the weapons he produced for the gods and heroes of the Tuatha Dé Danann were instrumental in their victories over their adversaries, such as the Fomorians, during the mythical battles that shaped the world. This aspect of his role highlights the importance of the blacksmith's craft in ancient Celtic society, not only in terms of warfare but also in its broader cultural and spiritual significance.

In addition to his prowess as a smith, Goibniu is also celebrated for his role in the feast of the gods, where he served as an ale-brewer. His ale was said to confer immortality upon the gods, further linking him to themes of sustenance, regeneration, and the eternal cycle of life and death.

Nuada Airgetlám

Nuada Airgetlám, often translated as "Nuada of the Silver Hand/Arm," is a prominent figure in Celtic mythology, particularly within the Irish tradition. He is revered as a king of the Tuatha Dé Danann, the pantheon of pre-Christian Irish gods, and is celebrated for his leadership, wisdom, and prowess in battle. Nuada's epithet "Airgetlám" refers to the silver hand or arm he received after losing his original limb in combat, a testament to the advanced skills in healing and craftsmanship attributed to the Tuatha Dé Danann.

Nuada's role as a leader of the Tuatha Dé Danann is central to his mythology. He is depicted as a just and noble king, leading his people through significant challenges, including the pivotal battles against the oppressive Fomorians, who represented chaos and destruction. Nuada's kingship was temporarily compromised when he lost his hand in the First Battle of Mag Tuired, as physical wholeness was a requirement for rulership among the Tuatha Dé Danann. However, after receiving his silver hand, crafted by the god of healing Dian Cecht and the god of craftsmanship Goibniu, he was reinstated as king, highlighting themes of restoration, resilience, and the interdependence of leadership and physical integrity in ancient Celtic society.

Welsh Mythology

Arawn

Arawn is a notable figure in Welsh mythology, particularly within the tales of the Mabinogi, a collection of medieval Welsh tales. He is known as the king of Annwn, the Otherworld, a realm of the dead and a place of enchantment, beauty, and abundance. Arawn's domain in Annwn is often depicted as a parallel to the earthly world, but free from suffering and death, reflecting ancient Celtic beliefs about the afterlife and the cyclical nature of life and death.

Arawn's most famous story involves his encounter with Pwyll, the prince of Dyfed, in the first branch of the Mabinogi. Arawn and Pwyll exchange places for a year and a day, allowing Pwyll to rule Annwn while Arawn takes Pwyll's place on Earth. This exchange is part of a plan to defeat Hafgan, Arawn's rival in Annwn, and through this, Pwyll earns Arawn's friendship and loyalty. Their exchange and the challenges they face highlight themes of friendship, loyalty, and the importance of understanding and respecting the sovereignty of other realms.

Arawn's role as the ruler of Annwn also associates him with themes of death, rebirth, and the supernatural. He is sometimes portrayed as a psychopomp, a guide for souls to the afterlife, reflecting his function as a bridge between the worlds of the living and the dead. His depiction in Welsh mythology emphasizes the nuanced view of the afterlife in Celtic beliefs, portraying Annwn not as a place of punishment, but rather as a realm of peace and eternal youth.

Rhiannon

Rhiannon is a prominent and enchanting figure in Welsh mythology, best known from the Mabinogi, a collection of medieval Welsh tales. Her character is often associated with horses and birds, and she embodies themes of sovereignty, the otherworldly, and subverted expectations of femininity and power. Rhiannon's most notable appearances are in the First and Third Branches of the Mabinogi, where her stories are woven with elements of magic, transformation, and profound challenges.

In the First Branch, Rhiannon is introduced as a beautiful and powerful woman who appears to Pwyll, the prince of Dyfed, on a magical horse that no one can catch. Pwyll eventually wins Rhiannon's hand in marriage, not through force or speed, but through respect and understanding. However, Rhiannon's story takes a tragic turn when her newborn son disappears under mysterious circumstances, leading to her unjust punishment. She is forced to carry visitors on her back as if she were a horse, a punishment she endures with dignity until her son is eventually returned to her.

In the Third Branch, Rhiannon marries Manawydan, and they, along with others, are cast into a mysterious enchantment that renders their land desolate. Rhiannon's wisdom and strength are again central to overcoming the challenges they face, highlighting her role as a figure of resilience and resourcefulness.

Rhiannon's character is often thought to have been inspired by earlier Celtic goddesses, particularly those associated with horses and sovereignty, such as Epona. Her portrayal in the Mabinogi blends elements of the divine and the human, creating a complex character who navigates the challenges of her life with grace and strength.

Cerridwen

Cerridwen is a powerful figure in Welsh mythology, often associated with magic, wisdom, transformation, and the cauldron of poetic inspiration. Her story is most famously recounted in the tale of Taliesin, where she embodies the roles of enchantress and mother. Cerridwen's cauldron, a central symbol in her mythology, is representative of the transformative power of magic and knowledge, as well as the cyclical nature of life, death, and rebirth.

In the tale, Cerridwen has two children: a beautiful daughter and a son, Morfran (also known as Afagddu), who is considered extremely ugly. Wishing to compensate for her son's appearance, Cerridwen decides to brew a potion in her magical cauldron to grant him the gift of wisdom and poetic inspiration. The potion must be boiled for a year and a day, and she enlists a young boy named Gwion Bach to stir the cauldron. However, a few drops of the potion spill onto Gwion's thumb as he stirs, and upon sucking his thumb, he receives the intended gifts meant for Morfran. Realizing what has happened, Gwion flees, and a shapeshifting chase ensues, with Cerridwen pursuing him. Eventually, Gwion transforms into a grain of wheat, and Cerridwen, now in the form of a hen, eats him, leading to her becoming pregnant and giving birth to Taliesin, the greatest poet of the Celtic Britons.

Branwen

Branwen, a figure from Welsh mythology, is one of the central characters in the "Mabinogi," specifically in the "Second Branch" of these medieval Welsh tales. She is a princess, the daughter of Llŷr and the sister of Brân the Blessed, a giant and king of Britain. Branwen's story is a tragic tale of love, diplomacy, and war, underscoring themes of betrayal, familial loyalty, and the consequences of political alliances.

Branwen's narrative begins when she is given in marriage to Matholwch, the king of Ireland, as part of a diplomatic alliance. However, this union, intended to forge a strong bond between Britain and Ireland, soon deteriorates due to treachery and disrespect towards Branwen and her family. In Ireland, Branwen is subjected to harsh treatment and is eventually reduced to the status of a kitchen slave as punishment for her brother Efnisien's insult to Matholwch, which involved mutilating Matholwch's horses as retribution for the perceived slight during the marriage negotiations.

Despite her suffering, Branwen demonstrates resilience and ingenuity. She trains a starling to carry a message across the Irish Sea to her brother Brân, informing him of her plight. This act sets in motion a series of events that lead to a devastating war between Ireland and Britain. Brân leads an expedition to rescue her, resulting in a catastrophic battle that decimates both sides. Branwen's story ends in heartbreak; she dies of grief upon returning to Wales, lamenting the destruction her marriage has wrought upon her homeland and Ireland.

Amaethon

Amaethon, in Celtic mythology, is a less prominently featured but significant deity, particularly within the Welsh tradition. He is known as the god of agriculture, responsible for the cultivation of the land and the care of crops, which underscores the ancient Celts' deep connection to the earth and the importance of agriculture in their society. As a divine figure, Amaethon embodies the nurturing aspects of the land, fertility, and the cycles of growth and harvest that sustain life.

One of the most notable stories involving Amaethon is his role in the mythical battle known as the Battle of the Trees, or Cad Goddeu, which is detailed in medieval Welsh poetry. According to legend, Amaethon steals a dog, a lapwing, and a roebuck from Arawn, the king of Annwn (the Otherworld), which leads to a great battle between the forces of Annwn and the deities of the earthly realm. Amaethon's theft and the ensuing conflict highlight themes of rivalry and the struggle for control over the natural world's vital resources.

The Battle of the Trees is particularly fascinating due to its magical aspects, where warriors are said to have been transformed from trees and plants into fighting men, through the enchantments of Gwydion, Amaethon's brother, who is a powerful magician and trickster figure in Welsh mythology. This transformation symbolizes the deep interconnection between the natural world and the human realm, as well as the power of magic and knowledge in shaping outcomes.

Gwydion

Gwydion is a central figure in Welsh mythology, renowned for his prowess as a magician, warrior, and trickster. He is a key character in the "Mabinogi," particularly in the Fourth Branch, which includes some of the most intricate and magical narratives of the medieval Welsh tales. Gwydion is a member of the divine family of Don, indicating his place within the pantheon of Welsh deities and heroes. His stories are rich with themes of magic, transformation, and the manipulation of fate, underscoring the complex interplay between human and divine actions in Celtic mythology.

One of Gwydion's most famous exploits involves his role in the birth and life of Lleu Llaw Gyffes, his nephew, whom he helps to raise and protect. Gwydion's ingenuity is showcased in his use of magic to overcome the curses placed upon Lleu by his mother, Arianrhod, who is Gwydion's sister. For instance, when Arianrhod declares that Lleu will not have a human name unless she gives it to him, Gwydion tricks her into naming Lleu. Similarly, he circumvents Arianrhod's curse preventing Lleu from bearing arms by creating an illusion that prompts her to unwittingly arm Lleu herself.

Another notable story involving Gwydion is his role in the Battle of the Trees, or Cad Goddeu, where he uses his magic to animate the trees and plants to fight against the forces of the underworld. This tale not only highlights

Gwydion's skill as a magician but also reflects the deep connection between the Celts and the natural world, with Gwydion acting as a conduit between the two.

Gwydion's tales often involve themes of transformation, both literal and metaphorical, as he navigates the challenges posed by the divine and mortal realms. His actions, sometimes morally ambiguous, contribute to the rich tapestry of Celtic mythology, where the boundaries between heroism and trickery, right and wrong, are frequently blurred.

Don

Don is a significant figure in Welsh mythology, known as a mother goddess and the matriarch of a divine family that includes many of the notable deities within the Welsh mythological pantheon. Her role and characteristics are somewhat analogous to those of Danu in Irish mythology, who is considered the mother of the Irish gods, the Tuatha Dé Danann. Don's family includes deities such as Gwydion, Arianrhod, and Lleu Llaw Gyffes, among others, each of whom plays crucial roles in the Welsh mythological narratives, particularly those found in the "Mabinogi," a collection of medieval Welsh tales.

Don herself is more of a background figure, with her presence implied through the actions and stories of her children. Unlike the more actively depicted deities, Don's influence is seen in the lineage and attributes of her offspring, who embody various aspects of the natural world, culture, and human endeavor. Her children are often involved in tales that explore themes of magic, craftsmanship, transformation, and the complex interplay between the mortal and divine realms.

Scottish Mythology

Cailleach

The Cailleach is a powerful and complex figure in Celtic mythology, often portrayed as a hag or crone embodying the forces of winter, death, and transformation. Her presence spans various Celtic cultures, with variations of her myth found in Scotland, Ireland, and the Isle of Man. The Cailleach is associated with the harshness of winter, the shaping of the landscape, and the sovereignty of the land, often representing the spirit of the wild and the embodiment of elemental forces.

In many stories, the Cailleach is depicted as a creator goddess who shaped the hills, mountains, and valleys, wielding a hammer with which she struck the earth to form the rugged landscapes. She is sometimes said to be the ancient ancestor of all gods and goddesses, a primordial figure from whom the natural world and its powers derive. Her connection to winter is profound; she is often described as bringing the snow and cold, ruling over the winter months from Samhain (the end of the harvest season) to Beltane (the beginning of summer), when her power wanes and she turns to stone or transforms into a young maiden, symbolizing the cycle of death and rebirth inherent in the changing seasons.

The Cailleach is also associated with deer, goats, and other wild animals, further emphasizing her role as a guardian of the wilderness and the cycles of nature. In some tales, she is the keeper of the Well of Youth, where she alone can renew her youth, reflecting themes of renewal, transformation, and the enduring power of the natural world.

Bride

Bride in Scottish mythology, is often associated with Brigid of Irish mythology, embodying similar attributes of fertility, poetry, craftsmanship, and healing. In Scotland, Bride is celebrated as a personification of spring and renewal, heralding the return of light and warmth after the harshness of winter. Her mythology intertwines with the changing seasons, agricultural practices, and the ancient festival of Imbolc, celebrated on February 1st, which marks the beginning of spring and is traditionally associated with Brigid in Ireland.

Scottish folklore often portrays Bride as a young maiden, symbolizing purity, renewal, and the potential for new life. She is celebrated during the time of Imbolc when the first signs of spring begin to emerge, and the power of the Cailleach, the embodiment of winter, starts to wane. According to some legends, the Cailleach, recognizing the arrival of spring, turns to stone on Imbolc, relinquishing her control over the land until the next winter, thus allowing Bride to bring forth the spring.

Bride's association with light and fire in Scottish mythology also reflects the ancient practice of lighting bonfires during Imbolc, symbolizing the return of the sun's warmth and the lengthening of the days. These fires were not only celebratory but also served as rituals of purification and healing, echoing Bride's role as a guardian of the hearth and a provider of spiritual and physical wellness.

Breton Mythology

Dahut (Ahes)

Dahut, also known as Ahes in some versions, is a mythical figure rooted in the legends of Brittany, a region in northwest France with a rich Celtic heritage. She is often associated with the city of Ys, a legendary city said to have been built below sea level and protected by a dam with a gate that Dahut was said to control. The story of Dahut and the city of Ys blends elements of Celtic mythology with local Breton folklore, creating a narrative rich in themes of hubris, temptation, and the power of nature.

According to legend, Dahut was the daughter of King Gradlon, a ruler of a land in Brittany, and a woman of otherworldly origins, often depicted as a sorceress or a fairy. Dahut is described as a beautiful and seductive figure, deeply associated with the sea and possessing magical abilities. She is credited with the construction of the city of Ys, which became a center of wealth, pleasure, and debauchery under her influence.

The downfall of Ys is central to Dahut's story. The legend recounts how Dahut's reckless behavior and disregard for the sea's power ultimately led to the city's destruction. She is said to have given the key to the city's gates to a lover, who, in some versions of the story, is the devil in disguise. The lover, or the devil, then opens the gates, allowing the sea to flood in and submerge the city, a symbol of divine or natural retribution for the city's and Dahut's excesses. In the aftermath of the catastrophe, Dahut is often portrayed as being transformed into a morgen or mermaid, doomed to dwell in the sea and haunt the coast of Brittany.

CHAPTER 2:

Other Characters from the Celtic Myths

In addition to the many deities featured in the Celtic myths, there are a range of other characters that play important roles. In this chapter, we'll introduce you to many of the notable characters from Celtic mythology that are not considered gods or goddesses. These include heroes, kings, queens, and other significant figures.

Irish Mythology

Cú Chulainn

Cú Chulainn is a legendary figure in Irish mythology, known for his extraordinary strength, skill, and heroism. He is a central character in the Ulster Cycle, one of the four main cycles of Irish mythological narratives. His birth name was Sétanta, but he gained the name Cú Chulainn, meaning "Culann's Hound," after he killed the ferocious guard dog of the smith Culann as a child and offered to take its place until a replacement could be reared. This act foreshadowed his future as a protector and warrior of unparalleled prowess.

Cú Chulainn's background is marked by supernatural elements, including his divine parentage; he is believed to be the son of the god Lugh and Deichtine, the sister of Conchobar mac Nessa, the king of Ulster. His training under the warrior woman Scáthach in Scotland, where he acquired his signature Gáe Bolg (a deadly spear), further cemented his legendary status. Cú Chulainn is best known for his central role in the epic tale "Táin Bó Cúailnge" (The

Cattle Raid of Cooley), where he single-handedly defends Ulster against the armies of Connacht led by Queen Medb. His tragic demise, foretold in prophecies, came about due to a series of geasa (sacred oaths) he broke, leading to his downfall. Cú Chulainn's life and death encapsulate themes of heroism, loyalty, and the tragic consequences of fate, making him a quintessential tragic hero of Irish mythology.

Fionn mac Cumhaill

Fionn mac Cumhaill is a celebrated hero in Irish mythology, central to the Fenian Cycle, also known as the Ossianic Cycle, which is a collection of stories narrating the adventures of Fionn, his warriors (the Fianna), and his descendants. Fionn's story blends myth, legend, and historical elements, making him a prominent figure in Irish folklore.

Fionn, the son of Cumhall, leader of the Fianna, and Muirne, was born under a veil of prophecy and danger, leading to a childhood in secrecy and exile to protect him from enemies of his slain father. His upbringing was marked by tutelage under various druids and warriors, most notably the wise woman and poetess Finneces, from whom he inadvertently gained the wisdom of the ages. This occurred when he accidentally tasted the Salmon of Knowledge, which was destined for Finneces. This event bestowed upon Fionn all of the world's knowledge, a key aspect of his legend.

As a warrior and leader, Fionn mac Cumhaill's exploits include defending Ireland from threats, both human and supernatural, and the pursuit of wisdom, justice, and honor. His tales often involve themes of loyalty, love, and the struggle against formidable adversaries. Fionn's charisma and wisdom, combined with his martial prowess, made him an archetypal hero, embodying the ideals of leadership and protection. His legacy includes not only his heroic deeds but also his role as a custodian of knowledge and culture, with many of his stories emphasizing the importance of wisdom over brute strength.

Oisín

Oisín is a significant figure in Irish mythology, renowned as a poet and warrior. He is best known as the son of Fionn mac Cumhaill, the legendary leader of the Fianna, and Sadhbh, a woman who was transformed into a deer by a dark druid's curse. Oisín's narrative is central to the Fenian Cycle, where he embodies the bridge between the heroic age of the Fianna and the Christian era in Ireland.

One of the most famous stories involving Oisín recounts his journey to Tír na nÓg, the mythical land of eternal youth, after falling in love with Niamh, a princess of this otherworldly realm. He travels with her to Tír na nÓg, leaving behind his father, Fionn, and the Fianna. In this land, Oisín experiences a timeless existence, untouched by age or sorrow. However, his longing for his homeland eventually compels him to return to Ireland, only to find that centuries have passed and all he knew has faded into legend.

Oisín's return is marked by tragedy and loss, symbolizing the transition from pagan traditions to a Christian Ireland. As he attempts to reintegrate, he accidentally breaks a geis (a taboo or prohibition), leading to his immediate aging and eventual death. Oisín's tales, particularly his dialogue with Saint Patrick, serve as a poignant narrative device, contrasting the heroic pagan past with the Christian present, and reflecting on themes of time, memory, and the inevitable change brought by the passage of eras.

Diarmuid Ua Duibhne

Diarmuid Ua Duibhne is a prominent figure in Irish mythology, celebrated for his valor and notable for his tragic love story. He is a member of the Fianna, a legendary group of warriors led by Fionn mac Cumhaill. Diarmuid is especially famous for his role in the Fenian Cycle of Irish mythology, where his life is marked by adventure, loyalty, and romance.

One of the most compelling aspects of Diarmuid's story is his love affair with Gráinne, who was betrothed to Fionn mac Cumhaill. On the night of their betrothal feast, Gráinne, struck by Diarmuid's beauty and bravery, places a geis upon him to elope with her, thus setting the stage for one of the most famous love triangles in Celtic lore. Despite his loyalty to Fionn, Diarmuid is bound by the geis and flees with Gráinne, leading to a series of pursuits and adventures as Fionn's men, and occasionally Fionn himself, seek to capture them.

Diarmuid is also known for his supernatural birthmarks, the "Love Spot," which made him irresistible to women, and his prowess in battle, enhanced by magical weapons. His tragic end comes during a boar hunt, which was prophesied at his birth. Despite Fionn's power to heal with water from his hands, a mix of jealousy, old grievances, and fate prevent Diarmuid from being saved, leading to his death and a lasting legacy of heroism tinged with sorrow.

Gráinne

Gráinne is a pivotal character in Irish mythology, known primarily for her central role in the tale of Diarmuid and Gráinne, which is part of the Fenian Cycle. She is the daughter of Cormac mac Airt, the High King of Ireland, making her a figure of significant status and influence in the mythological narratives. Gráinne is often portrayed as a symbol of beauty, desire, and autonomy, challenging the societal norms of her time.

Her story begins with her betrothal to Fionn mac Cumhaill, the aged leader of the Fianna, Ireland's band of heroic warriors. However, during the betrothal feast, Gráinne finds herself enchanted by the young and handsome Diarmuid Ua Duibhne, one of Fionn's most loyal warriors. Unwilling to marry Fionn and determined to follow her heart, Gráinne uses a geis, a compelling magical obligation, to persuade Diarmuid to elope with her, setting off a series of events that highlight themes of love, loyalty, and defiance.

The tale of Diarmuid and Gráinne's elopement and subsequent adventures is one of the most enduring love stories in Celtic mythology. It showcases Gráinne's complex character: her initial act of defiance against an arranged marriage, her enduring love and loyalty to Diarmuid through their years of hiding, and her cleverness and resourcefulness in evading capture.

Conchobar mac Nessa

Conchobar mac Nessa is a significant figure in Irish mythology, particularly within the Ulster Cycle, where he is depicted as the King of Ulster. His reign is marked by its central role in the epic narratives of this cycle, most notably in the "Táin Bó Cúailnge" (The Cattle Raid of Cooley). Conchobar's character is complex, embodying both noble and questionable traits, and his leadership is pivotal in the tales of the Ulster heroes, including the legendary warrior Cú Chulainn.

Conchobar's background is steeped in the intricate and often supernatural tapestry of Irish myth. He is said to be the son of Ness, a powerful woman who, through cunning and strategy, ensured that her son would become king. His father is often cited as Fachtna Fáthach, the previous King of Ulster, making Conchobar's claim to the throne both legitimate and divinely favored. Conchobar's rule is characterized by his efforts to maintain the sovereignty and prosperity of Ulster, often leading him into conflicts with other kingdoms and within his own court.

A notable aspect of Conchobar's reign is his association with the tragic hero Cú Chulainn, who is often portrayed as the king's nephew and foremost defender. Conchobar's decisions, particularly in the context of the "Táin Bó Cúailnge," highlight the complexities of kingship, including the burdens of leadership and the moral ambiguities faced by those in power.

Deirdre

Deirdre is a tragic heroine in Irish mythology, central to the Ulster Cycle, particularly in the story known as "The Tragedy of the Sons of Usnach" or "The Exile of the Sons of Uisliu." Her tale is one of love, beauty, and destiny, often compared to classical stories for its themes of fate and personal tragedy.

Deirdre's story begins with a prophecy at her birth, foretelling that she would grow to be a woman of stunning beauty, but that her beauty would bring great sorrow to Ulster. King Conchobar mac Nessa, upon hearing of her destined beauty, decides to rear her in seclusion, intending to marry her when she comes of age. However, Deirdre falls deeply in love with Naoise, one of the sons of Uisliu, a renowned warrior and member of the Ulster Cycle's heroic band, the Red Branch Knights.

Choosing love over the king's desires, Deirdre and Naoise, along with his brothers Ainle and Ardan, flee Ulster, seeking refuge in Scotland. Their tale is marked by the themes of passionate love and the pursuit of personal freedom, set against the backdrop of political intrigue and the harsh dictates of fate. Despite their efforts to evade destiny, Conchobar's machinations eventually lead to their tragic return to Ulster. Deirdre's story culminates in heartbreak and loss, as Naoise and his brothers are killed, fulfilling the dark prophecy that surrounded Deirdre's life.

Maeve (Medb)

Maeve (Medb) is a formidable queen in Irish mythology, primarily known from the Ulster Cycle, especially in the epic "Táin Bó Cúailnge" (The Cattle Raid of Cooley). As the queen of Connacht, Medb is portrayed as a powerful and independent ruler, known for her intelligence, political acumen, and sexual sovereignty. Her character embodies the complexities of sovereignty, warfare, and desire.

The most famous tale involving Medb centers on her determination to possess the Brown Bull of Cooley, which leads to a great war against the kingdom of Ulster. This desire to match and surpass the wealth of her husband, Ailill, in terms of possessing a bull as magnificent as his, underscores her competitive nature and quest for power. Medb's role in the epic highlights themes of rivalry, the dynamics of power, and the consequences of ambition. Medb's legacy in Celtic mythology is that of a complex character who defies simple categorization, embodying both the admirable and the cautionary aspects of power.

Ferdiad

Ferdiad is a notable figure in Irish mythology, particularly within the Ulster Cycle. He is best remembered for his tragic duel with Cú Chulainn in the epic "Táin Bó Cúailnge" (The Cattle Raid of Cooley). Ferdiad and Cú Chulainn are described as close friends and foster brothers, having trained together under the warrior woman Scáthach, where they formed a deep bond and became nearly equal in skill and prowess.

The climax of Ferdiad's story occurs when Queen Medb of Connacht manipulates him into fighting Cú Chulainn, who is single-handedly defending Ulster against her forces. Despite their close friendship, Ferdiad is compelled by loyalty to his queen and the promise of great rewards. The duel between Ferdiad and Cú Chulainn is one of the most poignant episodes of the Ulster Cycle, highlighting themes of loyalty, friendship, and the tragic consequences of war. It is a battle not only of physical strength but of emotional turmoil, as both warriors are reluctant to fight each other but are bound by their duties and allegiances.

Welsh Mythology

Pwyll

Pwyll, Prince of Dyfed, is a central character in Welsh mythology, particularly within the First Branch of the Mabinogi, an important medieval Welsh text. His story is notable for its themes of friendship, loyalty, and the interplay between the mortal world and the Otherworld, Annwfn.

Pwyll's most famous tale involves his encounter with Arawn, the king of Annwfn. In a display of respect and the bonds of friendship, Pwyll agrees to exchange places with Arawn for a year and a day to defeat Arawn's rival, Hafgan, without revealing their true identities. This adventure not only tests Pwyll's honor and courage but also cements a lasting alliance between Dyfed and Annwfn. Upon successfully completing this task and returning to his realm, Pwyll gains deep wisdom, supernatural allies, and the epithet "Pwyll, Head of Annwfn."

Another significant aspect of Pwyll's story is his relationship with Rhiannon, a powerful and enigmatic woman of the Otherworld, who becomes his wife. Their courtship and subsequent trials, including the mysterious disappearance of their son, Pryderi, add layers of complexity to Pwyll's character, depicting him as a figure capable of deep love, patience, and justice.

Manawydan

Manawydan, a key figure in Welsh mythology, is prominently featured in the Third Branch of the Mabinogi. He is the son of Llŷr, making him a brother to

Brân the Blessed and Branwen, and a central figure within this illustrious family of deities and heroes. Manawydan's story is notable for its exploration of themes such as loyalty, wisdom, and the quest for justice and restoration.

After the devastating war and events depicted in the Second Branch, which led to the deaths of Brân and Branwen, Manawydan returns to Britain with the few survivors. Despite being a rightful heir to the throne, he is denied kingship due to the ascendancy of another. His tale becomes intertwined with that of Pryderi, the son of Pwyll and Rhiannon, through Manawydan's marriage to Rhiannon and their subsequent adventures together.

Manawydan's character shines through his wisdom and restraint, particularly in the face of the mysterious enchantments that befall the land of Dyfed, leaving it desolate. Unlike tales that focus on martial prowess or magical feats, Manawydan's story emphasizes his intellect and diplomatic skills. He chooses cunning and patience over force to lift the enchantments, rescue Pryderi and Rhiannon from captivity, and restore prosperity to Dyfed.

Matholwch

Matholwch is a character from Welsh mythology, primarily featured in the Second Branch of the Mabinogi. He is the King of Ireland and becomes entwined with the British royal family through his marriage to Branwen, the sister of Brân the Blessed, the giant king of Britain. Matholwch's role in the narrative is pivotal, as his actions and the reactions to them set off a chain of events leading to tragic consequences.

The tale begins with Matholwch's arrival in Britain to seek Branwen's hand in marriage, an alliance that promises to unite Ireland and Britain and foster peace between the two realms. The initial hospitality and agreement to this union are marred by an act of violence from Efnisien, Branwen's half-brother, who mutilates Matholwch's horses in protest of the marriage. In an attempt to salvage the peace and the marriage alliance, Brân offers Matholwch compensation, including a magical cauldron that can resurrect the dead.

However, despite these reparations, the marriage sours due to the lingering resentment and mistrust stemming from the initial insult. Branwen's mistreatment at Matholwch's court and her subsequent plea for rescue lead to a devastating invasion by Brân and his forces.

Pryderi

Pryderi is a central figure in Welsh mythology, appearing prominently across several branches of the Mabinogi, which is among the most important and earliest prose literature of Wales. He is the son of Pwyll, Prince of Dyfed, and Rhiannon, a figure of otherworldly origins, making his lineage both royal and mystical. Pryderi's life, from his mysterious birth to his untimely death, is interwoven with magical events, heroic deeds, and the cultural and political tapestry of ancient Wales.

His story begins with his miraculous birth and disappearance as an infant, followed by his return and upbringing as a beloved child of the kingdom of Dyfed. Pryderi later inherits the rule of Dyfed from his father, Pwyll, and becomes a respected leader known for his prowess and generosity. His adventures include inheriting and losing magical swine, a gift from the Otherworld, which leads to conflict and his eventual capture in a war against another kingdom. Pryderi's character is marked by his strong ties to the land and its prosperity, as well as his deep connections to Welsh mythology's magical and otherworldly elements.

Taliesin

Taliesin is a legendary bard and poet in Welsh mythology, celebrated for his wisdom, prophetic abilities, and mastery of verse. His mythology is interwoven with historical elements, as he is also associated with the historical Taliesin, a poet who is believed to have lived in the 6th century and written praises for the kings of Brittonic kingdoms. The mythical Taliesin's story is most famously recounted in the tale of his magical transformation from Gwion Bach, a young boy, into Taliesin, the greatest poet of Britain.

The legend begins with Gwion Bach, who accidentally ingests three drops of a potion brewed by the witch-goddess Ceridwen, intended to bestow wisdom and inspiration upon her son. Upon tasting the potion, Gwion Bach instantly gains all knowledge and is pursued by Ceridwen. The chase involves a series of magical transformations, with Gwion and Ceridwen taking various forms. Eventually, Gwion transforms into a grain of wheat and is swallowed by Ceridwen, who was in the form of a hen. Ceridwen later gives birth to him as Taliesin, embodying a rebirth that grants him unparalleled poetic and prophetic powers.

Taliesin's role in Celtic mythology goes beyond his origin story. He is depicted as a figure of immense wisdom, capable of profound prophecies and possessing a deep understanding of the world. His poetry and tales, attributed to him over centuries, include themes of mysticism, heroism, and the natural and divine order.

Cornish Mythology

Tristan

Tristan is a legendary knight and tragic hero in the Arthurian tradition, which, while not strictly "Celtic mythology," is deeply influenced by Celtic themes, characters, and narratives. His story is most famously recounted in the romance "Tristan and Isolde," which has been adapted and retold through various cultures and eras. Tristan is often associated with the court of King Arthur, but his story predates and exists somewhat independently of the larger Arthurian cycle.

The tale of Tristan and Isolde is one of forbidden love and tragic circumstances. Tristan, a knight of Cornwall, is sent to Ireland to escort Isolde, a princess, back to Cornwall to marry his uncle, King Mark. Through a mix-up with a love potion, intended for Isolde and King Mark to ensure their love, Tristan and Isolde drink it instead and fall hopelessly in love with each other. Their passionate and illicit affair continues after Isolde's marriage to King Mark, leading to much turmoil, deceit, and heartache.

Tristan's character is marked by his prowess as a warrior, his loyalty to King Mark (which is in constant conflict with his love for Isolde), and his tragic fate, often dying from a wound received in battle or from despair when separated from Isolde. The story of Tristan and Isolde explores themes of love, honor, betrayal, and the inevitable tragedy that comes from their entwined destinies.

Iseult

Iseult, also known as Isolde, is a central figure in the legend of Tristan and Iseult, a tale of love and tragedy that

34

has become a cornerstone of Arthurian and medieval romance literature. Though the story is not part of Celtic mythology in the strictest sense, it is deeply influenced by Celtic legends and settings, particularly drawing from the rich tapestry of medieval Irish and Cornish traditions.

Iseult is most commonly portrayed as the princess of Ireland, renowned for her unmatched beauty and healing skills. She is betrothed to King Mark of Cornwall, but her fate takes a dramatic turn when she meets Tristan, King Mark's nephew and champion. Due to a misunderstanding involving a love potion, intended for her and King Mark, Iseult and Tristan fall deeply in love with each other, setting the stage for a complex and heartrending love triangle.

The character of Iseult embodies the conflict between duty and desire, as she is torn between her love for Tristan and her obligations as King Mark's queen. Her story is marked by themes of forbidden love, the struggle for happiness in the face of societal constraints, and the tragic consequences of fate and choices made under its influence.

CHAPTER 3:

The Branches of Celtic Mythology

Celtic mythology can be divided into different branches, primarily based on the geographical and linguistic distinctions within the Celtic cultures. While there are many similarities between these different branches, they each had their own unique languages, stories, characters, and myths.

Most of the myths included in this book come from the Irish branch of Celtic mythology, as that is the best known and most well documented. However, in this chapter, we'll share a bit of information about the different mythologies that combine to form what we now refer to broadly as "Celtic mythology".

Irish Mythology

Irish mythology is rich and diverse, and its stories are generally categorized into four main cycles, each with its own distinct themes and characters:

1) The Mythological Cycle

The Mythological Cycle in Irish mythology, also known as the Cycle of the Gods, delves into the ancient and enchanting realm of the Irish deities, primarily centering around the Tuatha Dé Danann, a race of god-like beings renowned for their proficiency in magic, druidry, and the arts. These tales, set in a time before the arrival of human beings in Ireland, unfold a world where magic, supernatural occurrences, and the exploits of divine beings intertwine to shape the landscape and destiny of Ireland.

Key narratives within this cycle include the arrival of the Tuatha Dé Danann in Ireland, descending through the clouds in a mist of enchantment, and their subsequent battles against other mythic races like the Fir Bolg and the fearsome Fomorians, led by the tyrant Balor. These stories are rich with themes of power struggles, magical prowess, and the intertwining fates of gods and mortals. The Lebor Gabála Érenn, or The Book of the Taking of Ireland, is a cornerstone of this cycle, presenting a mytho-historical narrative of the various peoples who settled in Ireland, from biblical times through the arrival and dominance of the Tuatha Dé Danann. Figures such as the Dagda, the father-figure god with control over life and death, and Lugh, the master of all arts and crafts, are prominent in these tales, symbolizing the ancient Irish reverence for nature, magic, and the otherworldly. This cycle, more than just a collection of myths, serves as a window into the spiritual and cultural fabric of early Irish civilization, reflecting a world where the divine and the earthly realm are inextricably linked.

2) The Ulster Cycle

The Ulster Cycle, set around the 1st century BC in the province of Ulster in ancient Ireland, is one of the most vibrant and action-packed segments of Irish mythology. It is primarily known for its tales of heroic deeds, fierce battles, and the tragic fates of its characters. The cycle's narrative is steeped in the ethos of a warrior society, where honor, bravery, and combat skills are paramount. The most celebrated tale of this cycle is the "Táin Bó Cúailnge" (The Cattle Raid of Cooley), which epitomizes the heroic and tumultuous nature of the cycle. This epic saga recounts the story of Queen Medb of Connacht and her husband Ailill, who plot to steal the prized brown bull of Cooley, leading to a ferocious war with the defenders of Ulster. Central to the Ulster Cycle is the figure of Cú Chulainn, a demigod-like warrior known for his extraordinary martial prowess, who single-handedly defends Ulster against Medb's forces.

The narratives of the Ulster Cycle also delve into themes of loyalty, duty, and the tragic consequences of pride and jealousy. The characters in these tales, from the mighty Cú Chulainn to the doomed Deirdre and the noble King Conchobar, are complex figures whose stories intertwine in a tapestry of war, love, betrayal, and supernatural intervention.

3) The Fenian Cycle

The Fenian Cycle, also known as the Fiannaíocht, is a captivating collection of tales from Irish mythology centered around the legendary hero Fionn mac Cumhaill and his band of warriors, the Fianna. Set in a time period roughly corresponding to the 3rd century, these stories blend elements of folklore, myth, and history to create a rich tapestry of adventure, magic, and heroism. Fionn, renowned for his wisdom, strength, and connection to the supernatural, emerges as a central figure, with the narrative detailing his rise from a young boy to the leader of the Fianna. His exploits include the acquisition of wisdom from the enchanted Salmon of Knowledge and battles against formidable foes, both human and otherworldly.

The Fenian Cycle also explores themes of loyalty, love, and betrayal, notably in the tale of Diarmuid and Gráinne, where Fionn's intended bride, Gráinne, falls in love with the young warrior Diarmuid. Their elopement leads to a dramatic chase and tragic consequences, embodying the cycle's exploration of the complex interplay between personal desire and societal duty. Unlike the Ulster Cycle, which focuses on the nobility and their heroic deeds, the Fenian Cycle is more concerned with the lives of common warriors and their interactions with the supernatural realm. This cycle is not just a collection of heroic narratives; it is a window into the culture and values of ancient Ireland, portraying a world where the lines between the natural and the supernatural are blurred, and where the ideals of bravery, wisdom, and loyalty are held in the highest esteem.

4) The Historical Cycle

The Historical Cycle, also known as the Cycle of the Kings, occupies a unique place in Irish mythology, blending elements of legend, myth, and historical fact. This cycle diverges from the purely mythological or heroic tales of the other cycles, focusing instead on semi-historical and legendary narratives of Irish kings and their realms. The stories are set in a more historical framework, tracing the lineage, deeds, and downfalls of various rulers of Ireland. A key feature of these tales is their blend of historical realism with mythological elements, creating a rich narrative fabric that straddles the line between history and legend.

One of the most renowned stories from this cycle is the tale of Brian Boru, an actual historical figure who rose to become the High King of Ireland and is famed for his leadership during the Battle of Clontarf against Viking invaders. The cycle also includes tales of lesser-known kings, their intrigues, battles for power, and interactions with the supernatural. While not as fantastical as the Mythological or Ulster Cycles, the Historical Cycle provides a valuable insight into the social and political structures of early Irish society, highlighting themes such as kingship, sovereignty, and the complex interplay of power, honor, and responsibility.

Welsh Mythology

Welsh mythology, a cornerstone of Celtic folklore, is a fascinating blend of ancient tales, deeply rooted in the cultural and mystical landscapes of Wales. The primary source of these myths is the "Mabinogion," a collection of eleven stories compiled from medieval Welsh manuscripts. The Mabinogion itself is divided into the Four Branches of the Mabinogi and several independent tales, many of which incorporate legendary figures and themes from Celtic mythology.

The Four Branches of the Mabinogi focus on a set of interconnected tales that include a wide range of characters, from kings and queens to magicians and mythical creatures. These stories are imbued with elements of magic, enchantment, and the traditional Celtic reverence for the natural world. They explore themes of love, betrayal, and the intertwining of fate and destiny. Notable among these are the tales of Pwyll, Prince of Dyfed, who exchanges places with the ruler of the Otherworld; Branwen, the daughter of Llŷr, whose tragic story involves a marriage alliance with Ireland that leads to war and devastation; and the story of Math and Gwydion, involving magic, transformation, and the creation of a woman from flowers.

In addition to the Mabinogi, the Mabinogion includes tales that are more clearly rooted in Arthurian legend, linking Welsh mythology with the wider body of British and European folklore. These stories showcase a world where the mystical and the mundane intersect, reflecting the deep connection of the Celtic people with the spiritual, natural, and supernatural realms.

Breton Mythology

Breton mythology, originating from Brittany in northwest France, is a captivating and unique strand of Celtic folklore that blends native Breton, French, and Celtic (especially Cornish and Welsh) mythological elements. Due to Brittany's geographical position and historical ties, its mythology has been influenced by both Celtic and Gallic traditions, resulting in a rich tapestry of legends and folklore.

A central feature of Breton mythology is its focus on the sea and forest, reflecting the region's strong maritime and rural heritage. The sea is often portrayed as a mysterious and otherworldly realm, inhabited by mystical creatures like the "Morgan" (mermaids) and the "Korrigan" (fairy-like spirits), who are said to enchant and interact with humans. The forests and wild lands of Brittany are also home to a variety of supernatural beings, from benevolent fairies to malevolent spirits.

One of the most famous legends in Breton mythology is that of the city of Ys, a mythical city said to have been swallowed by the sea. King Gradlon built the city for his daughter Dahut, who, according to legend, was responsible for its downfall due to her sins. Another notable aspect of Breton folklore is the "Ankou," a personification of death that is unique to the region, often depicted as a skeletal figure with a scythe.

Breton mythology also has overlaps with Arthurian legends, contributing to the rich tapestry of Arthurian folklore with stories that are unique to the region. These tales and legends have not only shaped the cultural identity of Brittany but also contributed to the broader canvas of Celtic mythology, offering tales of enchantment, mystery, and the close connection between the natural and supernatural worlds.

Scottish Mythology

Scottish mythology, infused with a distinctive blend of Celtic and Norse influences, forms a rich and diverse tapestry of folklore and legend. The rugged landscapes of Scotland, with its highlands, lochs, and islands, provide a dramatic backdrop for tales of mythical creatures, heroic figures, and ancient magic. A notable aspect of Scottish mythology is the presence of unique mythical creatures. The kelpie, a shape-shifting water spirit often taking the form of a horse, is a prominent figure in Scottish folklore, known for its malevolent trickery towards humans. Similarly, the selkie, seals that transform into humans, are central to Scottish island folklore, with tales often revolving around their interactions with, and sometimes marriages to, humans.

The stories also reflect the fusion of Celtic and Norse mythological traditions, a result of Scotland's history of both Celtic and Viking influence. This blend is evident in the various tales of heroes, battles, and supernatural beings. Legendary figures like Thomas the Rhymer, who was said to have the gift of prophecy after encountering the Queen of the Fairies, and the tragic tale of the lovers Deirdre and Naoise, which has parallels in Irish mythology, are part of Scotland's rich mythological heritage.

Scottish mythology also encompasses a wealth of ghost stories and local legends, many of which are tied to specific locations and historical events. Castles, battlefields, and ancient sites are often the settings for these tales, blending the historical with the supernatural.

Cornish Mythology

Cornish mythology, emanating from the southwestern tip of Britain in Cornwall, is a distinctive and enchanting subset of Celtic folklore, deeply intertwined with the broader tapestry of Celtic and Arthurian legends. Influenced by its unique geographical location and historical connections with Brittany and Wales, Cornish mythology blends local folklore with wider Celtic traditions, creating a rich narrative of myth and legend.

One of the most emblematic elements of Cornish mythology is its pantheon of fairy-like creatures and spirits. The "piskies" or pixies, small mischievous beings, are perhaps the most famous, often depicted as benevolent but playful entities that interact with humans in various ways. The tales of the Bucca, a spirit associated with the sea, reflect Cornwall's strong maritime heritage, embodying the respect and awe the Cornish people hold for the ocean and its mysteries.

Cornish mythology also shares in the wealth of Arthurian legend. Tintagel Castle in Cornwall is traditionally believed to be the birthplace of King Arthur, making the region central to many Arthurian tales. The story of Tristan and Iseult, a tale of tragic love, is another significant legend with strong Cornish ties.

Furthermore, the rugged Cornish landscape, with its moors, cliffs, and coastal areas, provides a dramatic setting for numerous local legends and ghost stories, often revolving around ancient stones, burial mounds, and historic landmarks.

Manx Mythology

Manx mythology, originating from the Isle of Man, a small island nestled between Great Britain and Ireland in the Irish Sea, presents a unique blend of Celtic and Norse influences, reflecting the island's rich historical tapestry. The mythology of the Isle of Man, often overshadowed by its Irish and Scottish counterparts, possesses its own distinctive charm and character, deeply rooted in the island's landscapes and cultural heritage.

Central to Manx mythology are the tales of fairies, known locally as the "Mooinjer veggey," often portrayed as powerful yet capricious beings who interact with the islanders in various ways. The Fairy Bridge on the island, for instance, is a testament to the local belief in these entities, with traditions requiring people to greet the fairies for good luck. Manx mythology also features a variety of unique creatures, such as the "Buggane," a fearsome ogre-like being, and the "Moddey Dhoo," a ghostly black dog haunting the halls of Peel Castle, embodying the island's affinity for ghostly and supernatural tales.

Additionally, the Norse influence is evident in the Manx mythology, reflecting the island's history as part of the Viking kingdom of the Isles. This blend of Celtic and Norse elements creates a rich narrative fabric, with stories of sea gods, mermaids, and warriors.

CHAPTER 4:

The Children of Lir

The tale of the Children of Lir is a deeply moving and complex narrative from Irish mythology, rich with themes of love, betrayal, endurance, and redemption, woven into the fabric of the mystical and magical landscape of ancient Ireland.

Lir, a prominent figure of the Tuatha Dé Danann—a supernatural race in Irish lore—was stricken with grief upon the death of his beloved wife. She left behind four children: Fionnuala, the eldest and only daughter, known for her wisdom and care for her younger brothers; Aodh, the gentle and kind-hearted; and the twins, Fiachra and Conn, who were full of life and mischief.

To mend the sorrow that had befallen Lir and to bring joy back into his life, the rulers of the Tuatha Dé Danann proposed that he marry again. They suggested Aoife, who was the sister of Lir's late wife and also a woman of considerable magical prowess. Initially, Aoife loved Lir and his children, and they lived together in harmony.

However, as time passed, a venomous seed of jealousy took root in Aoife's heart. She envied the deep affection that Lir had for his children, feeling sidelined and ignored. Her love turned into a bitter resentment, and she plotted to rid herself of the children.

On a journey with the children to visit their kin, Aoife led them to the edge of Lake Derravaragh. There, she used her sorcery to cast a malevolent spell, transforming the four siblings into swans. She condemned them to spend 300 years on Lake Derravaragh, 300 years on the stormy Sea of Moyle, and a final 300 years on the waters of Inis Glora. The spell could only be broken by the sound of a Christian bell, signifying the arrival of a new faith and the end of the dominance of the Tuatha Dé Danann in Ireland.

Despite their enchantment, the children retained their human consciousness and voices, which were hauntingly beautiful. They sang songs of such melancholy and beauty that all who heard them were moved to tears.

The news of this terrible deed spread quickly, and Aoife's treachery was exposed. As punishment for her actions, she was transformed into an air demon, doomed to wander the skies forever.

The years stretched into centuries as the children endured their fate. They faced the harshness of the Sea of Moyle's icy winds and storms, finding solace only in their unbreakable bond and the memories of their once-happy lives. Their final years on the Isle of Inis Glora were marked by a bittersweet peace, as they sensed the nearing end of their curse.

Finally, the day came when they heard the sweet sound of a Christian bell. Saint Patrick had arrived in Ireland, bringing with him the new faith that would release them from their enchantment. However, when the spell was broken, the long years caught up with them, and they returned to human form as ancient, withered figures. They were baptized by Saint Patrick before they passed away, leaving behind a legacy of resilience, the power of love, and the hope of redemption.

CHAPTER 5:

How Cú Chulainn Got His Name

The story of how Cú Chulainn, the preeminent warrior of Irish mythology, acquired his name is a tale rich with heroism, responsibility, and the transition from boyhood to legendary status. This narrative, deeply embedded within the Ulster Cycle—one of the four great cycles of Irish mythology—offers a glimpse into the early life of Sétanta, who would grow to become Cú Chulainn, a figure renowned for his unparalleled feats, valor, and the supernatural abilities that marked him as a demigod among mortals.

In the verdant, rolling hills of ancient Ulster, the young boy Sétanta, who was already showing signs of extraordinary talent and strength, was invited to a grand feast hosted by Culann, the kingdom's esteemed blacksmith. This blacksmith was not just any craftsman; his skills were unparalleled, and his forge produced weapons that were coveted across the land for their beauty and deadly effectiveness. The feast was to be attended by nobles, warriors, and druids, including Conchobar mac Nessa, the revered king of Ulster, under whose rule the kingdom flourished.

King Conchobar, setting out for the feast, extended the invitation to Sétanta, who was at that time engaged in a game of hurling with his peers. The sport, demanding both agility and strength, was a fitting pastime for the boy who was destined to become a legend. Sétanta eagerly accepted the invitation but requested to join the festivities later, as he wished to finish the game with his friends. Conchobar agreed and proceeded to Culann's stronghold, his mind preoccupied with matters of state and the anticipation of the evening's camaraderie.

Upon his arrival, Conchobar was swept into the feast's merriment, the warmth of the hall, the clinking of mead cups, and the bards' stirring tales, causing him to forget his promise to inform Culann of Sétanta's delayed arrival. Meanwhile, as dusk fell and the revelry reached its peak inside, Culann, seeking to secure his home for the night and protect his distinguished guests, unleashed his mighty hound. This was no ordinary dog; it was a beast of prodigious size and strength, its fierce loyalty to Culann matched only by its ferocity towards intruders.

When Sétanta approached Culann's estate, his heart light with anticipation, he was met not with welcome but with the thunderous growls and flashing teeth of the guard hound. The beast charged, and in that moment, Sétanta's youthful playfulness transformed into the resolve of a warrior. With no weapon but his hurley stick and sliotar (ball), he employed his hurling skills in a manner far removed from the games of his youth. With a precision that belied his age, he propelled the sliotar with such force into the gaping maw of the beast that it choked and ultimately perished. Other versions of the tale suggest he may have killed the dog with his bare hands or with a hurley stick.

The silence that followed was broken by the arrival of the feast's attendees, drawn by the commotion. Among them, Culann's grief at the loss of his protector was palpable, a loss that was deeply felt by all present, for the hound had been a guardian not only to Culann but to the community at large.

Sétanta, confronted with the gravity of his actions, stepped forward. In a voice that carried both regret and unwavering resolve, he offered to stand in the hound's stead, to protect Culann's household until such time as a new guardian could be raised. This gesture, remarkable for one so young, moved those who heard it. It was Cathbad, the wise druid, who then proclaimed that Sétanta would henceforth be known as Cú Chulainn, "the Hound of Culann," a name that would echo through the annals of Irish mythology, synonymous with honor, strength, and the complex interplay of youthful innocence and the responsibilities that come with emerging power.

CHAPTER 6:

The Cattle Raid of Cooley
(Táin Bó Cúailnge)

The Táin Bó Cúailnge, or "The Cattle Raid of Cooley," stands as a monumental epic within Irish mythology, woven into the rich tapestry of the Ulster Cycle. This saga, imbued with themes of valor, rivalry, and the tragic consequences of greed, unfolds across the verdant landscapes of ancient Ireland, where the realms of the mortal and the mystical intertwine.

At the heart of this narrative is Queen Medb of Connacht, a figure of formidable ambition and cunning. Her marriage to King Ailill, while politically advantageous, also breeds a competitive tension between the two monarchs. Their rivalry comes to a head in a moment of introspection, where they seek to measure their wealth and power against one another. Despite the vast treasures and resources at their disposal, they find themselves evenly matched in all but one regard: the possession of a magnificent bull. Ailill boasts ownership of Finnbennach, a splendid white-horned bull, while Medb lacks a counterpart of equal stature and renown.

Driven by a desire to eclipse her husband's status, Medb's gaze turns eastward to Ulster, where the majestic brown bull Donn Cúailnge resides, a creature whose fame and value know no equal. Determined to claim this prize and thus assert her supremacy, Medb embarks on a daring and ambitious campaign that will plunge the region into the throes of war.

Medb's call to arms resounds across the provinces, rallying a vast host under her banner. Notably absent from her coalition are the warriors of Ulster, cursed by the agonizing pangs of childbirth, a hex cast upon them by the goddess Macha as retribution for a past transgression. This incapacitation left the defense of Ulster in the hands of a single, remarkable champion: Cú Chulainn.

Cú Chulainn, a prodigy of martial prowess and the epitome of heroism, stands as the bulwark against Medb's encroaching forces. His legendary feats on the battlefield are marked by the invocation of single combat, a tradition that allows him to exploit the invaders' honor code and delay their advance. Through a series of duels, Cú Chulainn thins the ranks of Medb's champions, each encounter showcasing his skill, strategic acumen, and the supernatural fury of his battle frenzy, known as the ríastrad or "warp spasm."

Yet, the narrative is not solely defined by Cú Chulainn's martial exploits. Interwoven are tales of deception, diplomacy, and the complexities of kinship and loyalty. Medb, ever resourceful, employs a multitude of strategies to undermine Ulster's resistance, from negotiation and bribery to outright treachery. Among the most poignant episodes is the forced confrontation between Cú Chulainn and his foster brother, Ferdiad, a battle that epitomizes the epic's recurring motifs of divided loyalties and the personal cost of war.

As Queen Medb's forces pressed into Ulster, she became increasingly aware of the need to neutralize Cú Chulainn, who was single-handedly holding back her army through his heroic exploits. Recognizing the deep bond between Ferdiad and Cú Chulainn, Medb saw an opportunity to exploit this relationship. She employed a combination of flattery, manipulation, and promises of wealth and land to persuade Ferdiad to face Cú Chulainn in combat.

Despite his deep reluctance and the knowledge that he would be facing his dear friend, Ferdiad was eventually swayed by Medb's persuasions and the pressures of honor and duty that were paramount in the warrior culture of the time. The stage was set for a tragic confrontation at the ford that would be remembered as one of the most heartrending moments in all of Celtic mythology.

The battle between Ferdiad and Cú Chulainn lasted for three grueling days, with neither warrior willing to yield. On the first day, they fought with spears, on the second with swords, and on the third, they resorted to a ferocious hand-to-hand combat. Throughout the fight, both warriors displayed not only their unparalleled skill and bravery but also their deep mutual respect and sorrow at having to fight one another. The battle was marked by moments of poignant reflection on their past friendship and the cruel twist of fate that had turned them into adversaries.

Cú Chulainn, renowned for his supernatural warrior abilities, was ultimately forced to use the Gáe Bolga, a deadly weapon given to him by Scáthach, the formidable warrior woman who had trained both Cú Chulainn and Ferdiad as youths. This weapon was one that he had hoped never to use against Ferdiad. The Gáe Bolga was thrown into the water and summoned through a feat of skill to strike Ferdiad from below, inflicting a mortal wound.

As Ferdiad lay dying, the full tragedy of the situation unfolded. Cú Chulainn was overcome with grief, lamenting the loss of his friend and the circumstances that had led to their fatal duel. He cradled Ferdiad's head in his lap, mourning the passing of not only a great warrior but a cherished friend whose death marked one of the darkest moments in Cú Chulainn's own life.

As the narrative progresses, Cú Chulainn's battles continue, but his spirit and body are wearied by the relentless combat and the emotional toll of Ferdiad's death. Queen Medb, recognizing that Cú Chulainn's resistance cannot be overcome by force alone, employs various strategies to circumvent him, including magic, deceit, and attempts to negotiate.

Eventually, the men of Ulster begin to recover from the curse that had incapacitated them, allowing them to rally and come to Cú Chulainn's aid. This marks a turning point in the conflict, as the Ulster warriors, led by their king, Conchobar mac Nessa, and other notable champions, join the fray, shifting the balance of power.

The climax of the Táin comes with the actual cattle raid, where the Connacht forces, despite facing fierce resistance, manage to capture the Donn Cúailnge and begin driving it back to Connacht. However, the story does not end with a simple victory for Medb. The brown bull of Cooley, upon being brought into Connacht, engages in a fierce battle with Ailill's white-horned bull, Finnbennach. The two beasts fight a tumultuous and destructive battle that traverses much of the landscape, symbolizing the widespread ruin and futility of the conflict initiated by Medb's ambition.

In the end, the Donn Cúailnge defeats Finnbennach but is mortally wounded in the process. The brown bull, embodying the pride and spirit of Ulster, dies of its wounds, leaving a trail of destruction in its wake. This outcome serves as a somber reflection on the cost of greed and the pursuit of power, highlighting the senseless loss and devastation that result from such conflicts.

The Táin Bó Cúailnge concludes with the armies disbanding and the warriors returning to their homes, bearing the scars of battle and the weight of their experiences. The epic, through its intricate narrative and complex characters, offers profound insights into the nature of heroism, the bonds of loyalty, and the tragic consequences of human desires and conflicts, leaving a lasting impact on Irish literary and cultural heritage.

CHAPTER 7:

The Salmon of Knowledge

The myth of the Salmon of Knowledge is a captivating tale from Irish mythology that intertwines fate, wisdom, and the transformative power of knowledge. This story, deeply embedded in the cultural tapestry of Ireland, serves as a prelude to the legendary exploits of Fionn mac Cumhaill, a central figure in Irish folklore known for his leadership of the Fianna, his wisdom, and his prowess as a warrior and poet.

The narrative unfolds along the banks of the River Boyne, a place teeming with ancient magic and mysticism. Here resides Finnegas, a druid of great renown, steeped in the lore and the druidic arts, who has dedicated his life to the pursuit of a singular quest—the capture of the Salmon of Knowledge, also known as the Bradán Feasa. This was no ordinary salmon; it was imbued with all the world's knowledge, having consumed the hazelnuts from the nine hazel trees of wisdom that grew around the Well of Segais. The nuts from these trees fell into the well, where they were eaten by the salmon, thus transferring to it the sacred wisdom contained within.

Finnegas knew that whoever first tasted the flesh of this salmon would inherit its vast knowledge, and so he fished patiently in the waters of the Boyne, yearning for the day he would catch the elusive fish. His days were spent in a blend of meditation, teaching, and fishing, creating a life that was a testament to the druidic balance of action and contemplation.

Enter young Fionn mac Cumhaill, who comes under Finnegas's tutelage not by chance but by a series of fateful events that hint at the young boy's destined greatness. Fionn, the posthumous son of Cumhall, leader of the Fianna, and Muirne, was sent to Finnegas for guidance and education, a common practice among the nobility and warrior class of the Celts, where fostering out children to learn various arts was a tradition.

Fionn's time with Finnegas was marked by learning the skills of hunting, poetry, and the druidic arts, but his life was about to change profoundly the day Finnegas finally caught the Salmon of Knowledge. Finnegas, recognizing the momentous nature of this catch, entrusted Fionn with the task of cooking the salmon but sternly instructed him not to eat any part of it, for the wisdom it contained was the culmination of Finnegas's lifelong quest.

As Fionn tended to the cooking of the salmon, his attention never wavered, his thoughts perhaps wandering to the lessons he had learned and the future that lay ahead of him. But fate intervened when he accidentally burned his thumb on the salmon's hot skin. Instinctively, Fionn brought his thumb to his mouth to ease the pain, and in that seemingly insignificant act, the course of his life was altered. The wisdom of the salmon, which was meant for Finnegas, flowed into Fionn, illuminating his mind with the knowledge and insights of the ages.

Finnegas, upon realizing what had transpired, saw the hand of destiny at work. Though he had longed for the wisdom of the salmon, he recognized that Fionn was its intended recipient. With a mix of resignation and acceptance, he instructed Fionn to finish the salmon, thereby completing the transfer of knowledge.

From that day forward, Fionn mac Cumhaill possessed an unparalleled wisdom that would aid him in his many adventures and challenges. By biting his thumb, he could draw upon the salmon's wisdom, a gift that would lead him to become one of the most revered figures in Irish mythology.

CHAPTER 8:

The Myth of Oisín and Tír na nÓg

The myth of Oisín and Tír na nÓg is one of the most enchanting and poignant tales from Celtic mythology, particularly within the body of literature associated with the Fenian Cycle, which revolves around the hero Fionn mac Cumhaill, his warriors the Fianna, and his son Oisín. This story intertwines themes of love, adventure, and the yearning for a land beyond the constraints of time and age, Tír na nÓg, which translates to "The Land of the Young."

The tale begins with Oisín, a renowned poet and warrior of the Fianna, encountering a mysterious and beautiful woman while hunting with his companions. This woman, Niamh of the Golden Hair, is a princess from the magical realm of Tír na nÓg, a place where time stands still, and inhabitants never age or suffer. She tells Oisín of her love for him and invites him to return with her to her homeland, promising a life of eternal youth, joy, and peace, free from the sorrows and toils of the mortal world.

Captivated by Niamh's beauty and the allure of Tír na nÓg, Oisín agrees to accompany her. They journey across the sea on a magical steed that can travel over water as if it were land, arriving in a land of unparalleled beauty and splendor. Oisín is welcomed into this enchanting realm, where he experiences the joys and wonders of Tír na nÓg, spending what seems to him like a few short years filled with happiness and love.

However, as time passes, Oisín begins to yearn for his homeland and his father, Fionn mac Cumhaill. He wishes to return to Ireland, if only to visit and see his kin once more. Niamh, understanding his longing but warning him of the passage of time in the mortal world, grants him his wish to return on the condition that he must not set foot on the soil of Ireland, for centuries have passed since his departure, and to touch the ground would mean yielding to the mortal fate of aging.

Oisín sets out on the same magical steed that brought him to Tír na nÓg, but upon reaching Ireland, he finds a land changed beyond recognition. The once mighty Fianna and his father are long gone, replaced by a world that has moved on without him. As he encounters the people of this new Ireland, they marvel at the sight of this imposing warrior from a bygone era.

Tragedy strikes when Oisín attempts to help some men who are struggling to move a heavy stone. As he leans from his horse to lift the stone, his saddle girth breaks, causing him to fall to the ground. The moment he touches the earth, the centuries catch up with him, and he is transformed into an ancient, withered man, his years in Tír na nÓg undone in an instant.

The story of Oisín's return and subsequent transformation spreads throughout the land, reaching the ears of Saint Patrick, who visits the now elderly Oisín. In their conversations, Oisín recounts his adventures in Tír na nÓg and the glory days of the Fianna, providing a poignant contrast between the pagan past and the Christian present, between the ephemeral joys of Tír na nÓg and the inevitable passage of time in the mortal world.

CHAPTER 9:

The Legend of Tristan and Iseult

The legend of Tristan and Iseult, a cornerstone of Celtic and Arthurian mythology, is a rich tapestry of love, intrigue, and tragedy that unfolds against the backdrop of medieval Europe. Its narrative complexity and emotional depth have cemented its place in the annals of romantic literature, inspiring countless adaptations and interpretations.

Tristan, a valiant knight of Cornwall, is tasked by his uncle, King Mark, to escort the Irish princess Iseult back to Cornwall to become Mark's bride. The alliance through marriage is meant to cement peace between the two realms, following Tristan's heroic victory over the Irish champion Morholt, who had been exacting tribute from Cornwall. Iseult is renowned not only for her surpassing beauty but also for her healing abilities, which she uses to cure Tristan of the wounds inflicted by Morholt, thereby intertwining their fates even before the fateful journey to Cornwall.

The pivotal turn in their story occurs during their voyage from Ireland, when Tristan and Iseult inadvertently consume a love potion intended for Iseult and King Mark. The potion, crafted by Iseult's mother and meant to ensure a loving union between Iseult and Mark, instead forges an indissoluble bond of passionate love between Tristan and Iseult. This love, both transcendent and cursed, becomes the crucible for their ensuing trials and tribulations.

Despite the potion's effects, Iseult's duty to marry King Mark is inescapable, and their secret love becomes a source of both exquisite joy and profound torment. They engage in a clandestine affair, fraught with the risk of discovery and the moral turmoil of their betrayal. Their love is a constant dance of proximity and separation, as circumstances force them to part ways only to find each other again, as if by destiny.

One of their most significant separations occurs when their affair is discovered. Tristan is forced into exile, a consequence of their betrayal of King Mark's trust. During his exile, Tristan travels to Brittany, where he encounters Iseult of the White Hands, a woman of noble birth who bears a striking resemblance to his true love. Compelled by her resemblance to Iseult of Ireland and the political advantages of the match, Tristan marries her, yet he remains emotionally and spiritually bound to Iseult of Ireland, rendering him incapable of consummating his marriage to Iseult of the White Hands.

Tristan's life in Brittany is marked by a restless spirit and a yearning for his lost love. He engages in heroic deeds and quests, perhaps in an attempt to distract himself from his sorrow or to prove his enduring valor. However, the shadow of his love for Iseult of Ireland looms large over his existence, casting a pall over his achievements and his marriage to Iseult of the White Hands.

The culmination of Tristan and Iseult's tragic saga is precipitated by Tristan's mortal wounding by a poisoned lance. Knowing that only Iseult of Ireland possesses the skill to heal him, Tristan sends for her in desperation. He instructs his loyal servant to hoist a white sail upon her arrival, signaling her presence, or a black sail if she is not on the ship. Iseult of the White Hands, consumed by jealousy and bitterness over Tristan's undying love for another, deceives Tristan about the color of the sail, claiming it is black.

Tristan, heartbroken by the belief that Iseult of Ireland has forsaken him, succumbs to his despair and injuries, dying just as Iseult of Ireland arrives. Iseult's grief upon finding Tristan dead is profound, a testament to the depth of their love and the cruelty of their fate. In some versions of the story, Iseult of Ireland dies of grief beside Tristan, their lives and deaths inextricably intertwined.

CHAPTER 10:

The Pursuit of Diarmuid and Gráinne

The Pursuit of Diarmuid and Gráinne is a prominent tale from Irish mythology, part of the Fenian Cycle, which centers around the legendary hero Fionn mac Cumhaill and his band of warriors, the Fianna. This story weaves together themes of love, loyalty, betrayal, and destiny, and it remains one of the most enduring and captivating narratives in Celtic lore.

The tale begins with the aging Fionn mac Cumhaill, who, having been widowed twice, decides to marry again. He seeks the hand of Gráinne, the beautiful daughter of Cormac mac Airt, the High King of Ireland. Gráinne, however, is much younger than Fionn and feels no love for him. During the betrothal feast, she lays eyes on the handsome and gallant Diarmuid Ua Duibhne, one of Fionn's most trusted warriors, and falls deeply in love with him.

Gráinne, using a sleeping potion, puts all the guests at the feast to sleep, except for Diarmuid. She then places a geis upon Diarmuid, a kind of inviolable obligation or taboo in Celtic mythology, compelling him to elope with her. Diarmuid is torn between his loyalty to Fionn, his leader and foster father, and his growing affection for Gráinne. Initially, he refuses Gráinne's advances, citing his loyalty to Fionn, but the power of the geis and Gráinne's entreaties eventually compel him to comply. Bound by the geis placed upon him, Diarmuid is compelled to take her away from Tara, thus igniting the fury of Fionn and setting the stage for a relentless pursuit across Ireland.

As the narrative unfolds, Diarmuid and Gráinne navigate through a labyrinth of trials and tribulations, their journey emblematic of the archetypal hero's quest, fraught with symbolic and literal obstacles. They traverse dense forests, cross raging rivers, and scale formidable mountains, each landscape imbued with its own mystical challenges and guardians.

One of the most notable trials they face is their encounter with the Aonbhar of the Flowing Mane, a magical steed that can traverse both land and water with unmatched speed. Diarmuid, with his unparalleled prowess, manages to tame the beast, securing a swift and tireless ally in their flight from Fionn's relentless pursuit.

In another gripping episode, they seek refuge in the realm of the Sidhe, the ancient Irish gods and spirits of the land. Here, they are granted sanctuary by Aengus Óg, the god of love and youth, who shelters them within the otherworldly confines of his domain, hidden from the prying eyes of Fionn and the mortal world. This interlude in the Sidhe offers a brief respite from their trials, enveloping them in an enchantment that momentarily suspends the harsh realities of their predicament.

Throughout their journey, the couple encounters various figures from Celtic mythology, each presenting their own challenges or offering aid. The benevolent giantess Benandonner provides them with shelter and counsel, her immense strength and wisdom proving invaluable against the threats that stalk them.

Despite these trials, Diarmuid's unwavering bravery and Gráinne's cunning continually thwart Fionn's efforts to recapture them. Their love deepens with each ordeal, forging an unbreakable bond that transcends the physical hardships of their plight.

The tale reaches its tragic climax when Diarmuid, despite being under the protection of the god Aengus Óg, meets his fate during a boar hunt. Diarmuid, who is fated to be killed by a boar according to a prophecy from his youth, participates in the hunt at Fionn's behest. He is gored by the boar and, as he lies dying, begs Fionn to use his magical powers to heal him. Fionn, who possesses the ability to heal with water carried in his hands, initially refuses, still bitter over Diarmuid's betrayal. Though Fionn is eventually persuaded to help, he lets the water slip through his fingers twice. By the time he decides to save Diarmuid on the third attempt, it is too late.

Diarmuid's death marks the end of the pursuit, leaving Gráinne heartbroken. The tale concludes with Gráinne returning to Fionn, but the story of her elopement with Diarmuid remains a poignant testament to the themes of love's triumph and tragedy, the complexities of loyalty and honor, and the inexorable pull of destiny. The Pursuit of Diarmuid and Gráinne is celebrated for its rich narrative, complex characters, and the depiction of the timeless struggle between personal desire and societal duty.

CHAPTER 11:

The Story of Culhwch and Olwen

The story of Culhwch and Olwen, from the collection of medieval Welsh tales known as the Mabinogion, is a rich tapestry of myth, magic, and adventure, interwoven with the themes of love, loyalty, and the quest for the seemingly unattainable.

The narrative begins with the birth of Culhwch, the son of King Cilydd by his wife, Goleuddydd. After Goleuddydd's tragic death, which occurs following a peculiar incident involving a herd of swine, King Cilydd remarries. His new wife, desiring that her own son be the heir to Cilydd's kingdom, suggests that Culhwch should marry her daughter. Culhwch, however, rejects this proposal, an act that angers his stepmother. In retaliation, she places a curse on Culhwch, dooming him to marry only Olwen, the daughter of the giant Ysbaddaden Pencawr, whom she believes to be impossible to court due to her father's dangerous nature and the prophecy surrounding his death.

Olwen is no ordinary maiden; she is famed for her beauty and the supernatural phenomenon that white clovers spring up beneath her feet with each step she takes. Despite knowing little about Olwen or her whereabouts, Culhwch is compelled by the curse and his burgeoning desire to seek her out. This quest leads him to the court of his cousin, King Arthur, where Culhwch invokes the right of kinship and requests Arthur's aid in his quest.

Arthur, moved by family loyalty and the adventurous spirit of the task, assembles a group of his finest warriors to assist Culhwch. This band includes some of the most celebrated figures in Arthurian legend, such as Kei (Kay), known for his sharp tongue and strength; Bedwyr (Bedivere), who is unparalleled in his swiftness and skill in combat; and other notable knights, each possessing unique abilities and attributes that contribute to the quest.

The group sets out to find Olwen and comes upon her in her father Ysbaddaden's fortress. Culhwch and Olwen's meeting is marked by instant mutual affection, but their path to union is obstructed by Ysbaddaden himself. The giant, aware of the prophecy that his death will coincide with Olwen's marriage, seeks to prevent this outcome by imposing a series of seemingly insurmountable tasks upon Culhwch. Here, we delve into these challenges, providing the background and intricacies involved in each:

Capturing Twrch Trwyth: The central and most perilous task involves capturing Twrch Trwyth, an otherworldly boar of immense power and malevolence, once a prince but transformed by a curse. Ysbaddaden demands Culhwch retrieve specific items from the boar: a comb, shears, and a razor, which are magically held between its ears. The hunt for Twrch Trwyth becomes an epic undertaking, requiring Culhwch to enlist the aid of King Arthur and his legendary knights. This fearsome chase spans across the countryside, confronting the hunters with various dangers and leading to many fierce skirmishes with the boar and its offspring.

Rescuing Mabon ap Modron: To successfully hunt Twrch Trwyth, Culhwch needs the best hound in the world, Drudwyn, which can only be handled by Mabon ap

Modron. However, Mabon was kidnapped from his mother three nights after his birth and is imprisoned in a mysterious, unknown location. To find and rescue Mabon, Culhwch's companions seek out the oldest animals in the world, each one leading them to an older creature, until they are guided by the ancient salmon of Llyn Llyw to Mabon's prison. The rescue of Mabon is crucial, as his expertise as a huntsman and his ability to handle Drudwyn are indispensable for the hunt of Twrch Trwyth.

Obtaining the Horses of Gweddw: Another task set by Ysbaddaden is for Culhwch to procure the horses of Gweddw, a ruler who possesses magnificent horses known for their incredible speed and strength. These horses are essential for Culhwch and his allies to keep pace with the Twrch Trwyth and to endure the arduous journey and battles that lie ahead.

Retrieving the Cauldron of Diwrnach the Irishman: Culhwch is tasked with obtaining a magical cauldron belonging to Diwrnach, a fierce Irishman. This cauldron has the unique property of boiling food only for the brave, making it a symbol of valor. Culhwch and his companions must travel to Ireland, where they initially attempt to negotiate with Diwrnach. When diplomacy fails, they are forced to engage in battle, showcasing their martial prowess to secure the cauldron.

Cutting the Beard of Dillus the Bearded: Ysbaddaden requires the beard of Dillus the Bearded to create a leash for the hound Drudwyn, critical for the hunt. Dillus, however, is a formidable giant, and his beard can only be cut while he is alive. This task demands a blend of cunning and combat skill, as Culhwch's party must subdue Dillus without causing his death, to cut his beard.

Hunting the Ysgithyrwyn Chief Boar: In addition to Twrch Trwyth, Culhwch must hunt another mystical boar, Ysgithyrwyn Chief Boar. Ysbaddaden requires the tusk of this boar for his personal grooming in preparation for Olwen's wedding. This task, while mirroring the hunt for Twrch Trwyth, presents its own unique set of challenges and dangers, underscoring the perilous nature of Culhwch's quest.

Retrieving the Harp of Teirtu: Ysbaddaden's tasks also include obtaining the Harp of Teirtu, a magical instrument that plays itself, captivating anyone who hears its music. The task likely involves overcoming the magical protections surrounding the harp and convincing or compelling Teirtu to part with this enchanting item.

With the tasks fulfilled, Culhwch returns to Ysbaddaden, not just as a suitor but as a formidable force who has proven his worth and cunning by accomplishing what was thought to be impossible.

Ysbaddaden, who had set these tasks hoping they would lead to Culhwch's demise, is now faced with the inevitability of his own prophesied fate. The giant had long known that his death would be intertwined with his daughter's marriage, and Culhwch's success signifies that his end is near. In a final act of compliance or perhaps resignation, Ysbaddaden submits to the fulfillment of the prophecy.

As part of the wedding preparations, Ysbaddaden instructs Culhwch and his companions to give him a final grooming, a task that includes trimming his hair, beard, and nails. This grooming, however, serves as a symbolic gesture, signifying Ysbaddaden's acceptance of his fate and the transition of Olwen from his guardianship to her new life with Culhwch. During this process, in a blend of ceremonial act and execution, Ysbaddaden's head is cut off, thus fulfilling the prophecy tied to Olwen's marriage.

With Ysbaddaden's death, the last obstacle to Culhwch and Olwen's union is removed. The tale culminates in their marriage, a joyous and celebratory event that not only marks the union of two lovers but also symbolizes the triumph of perseverance, love, and heroism over seemingly insurmountable odds. The wedding is celebrated with great festivity, attended by Culhwch's allies, including the renowned King Arthur and his knights, who had played pivotal roles in assisting Culhwch throughout his quest.

CHAPTER 12:

The Wooing of Étaín

The Wooing of Étaín (or "Tochmarc Étaíne" in Irish) is one of the most celebrated and intricate tales from the Irish Mythological Cycle, specifically from the Ulster Cycle of tales. It weaves together themes of love, transformation, rebirth, and the enduring nature of the soul across lifetimes. The story is rich with supernatural elements, reflecting the deep connection between the human and the divine in Celtic mythology.

Étaín, a woman of unparalleled beauty, was like a beacon of light that drew the gaze of both mortal and divine alike. Her grace was such that it transcended the bounds of the human world, capturing the heart of Midir, a noble member of the Tuatha Dé Danann. Midir, struck by the depth of his love for Étaín, sought her companionship, and in the fullness of time, they were united, their hearts entwined in a love as pure as it was deep.

Yet, in the shadows of this love, jealousy took root. Fuamnach, Midir's first wife, viewed Étaín not as a fellow soul but as a rival to be vanquished. Consumed by envy, Fuamnach called upon her dark arts, casting a spell that transformed Étaín into a shimmering pool of water, erasing her human form from the world. But such was Étaín's purity and resilience that from the waters, she re-emerged, first as a worm and then, transcending this humble form, she became a magnificent purple fly. In this new guise, Étaín's beauty was undiminished, and her presence was a source of joy and comfort to those around her, her wings creating music that soothed all who heard it.

Yet, Fuamnach's malice was unyielding, and she sought to banish Étaín further still. A great wind was summoned, scattering Étaín to the far corners of the land, until at last, she found herself in the hall of Eochaid Airem, the High King of Ireland. Eochaid, enchanted by the beautiful fly that seemed to bring light and music into his hall, grew to cherish her presence. Fate, however, had yet another twist in store. Étaín, in her fly form, fell into a cup of wine and was swallowed by Eochaid, only to be reborn once more, this time as a human, emerging from the earth as the most radiant woman in all of Ireland, with no memory of her past lives.

Eochaid, beholding Étaín's beauty anew, took her as his queen, and for a time, they knew happiness. But the bonds of true love, once formed, are not so easily broken. Midir, whose heart had never strayed from Étaín, sought her out, determined to reclaim his lost love. Presenting himself at Eochaid's court, Midir challenged the king to a series of games.

The games, traditional in nature, likely involved feats of strength, skill, and strategy—tests of might such as wrestling or swordplay, challenges of skill like archery or horse racing, and contests of wit and strategy, perhaps akin to the ancient Irish board game of fidchell, which was similar to chess.

As the contests commence, Eochaid and Midir engage in these games, the court watching with bated breath as two formidable opponents match each other in prowess and guile. Midir, however, is no mere mortal; his heritage imbues him with abilities that far surpass human limitations. Despite Eochaid's valor and kingly might,

Midir bests him at every turn, his victories a testament to the otherworldly power that courses through his veins.

Midir, having proven his superiority, makes a bold wager: if he wins this last contest, he shall be granted a boon by Eochaid. The king, bound by honor and the customs of hospitality and fair play, agrees, unaware of the depth of Midir's desire and the lengths to which he will go to reclaim Étaín.

With the stakes set, the final game unfolds, a contest of skill that demands not just physical prowess but a keen mind and indomitable spirit. The details of this game are shrouded in the mists of legend, but it is said that Midir's victory was as swift as it was decisive, a feat that left no room for doubt or dispute.

In the moment of his triumph, Midir reveals the true purpose of his visit and the nature of his desired boon: a kiss from Étaín, the queen herself. The court is stunned, and Eochaid, caught between the rock of his promise and the hard place of his honor, consents, albeit reluctantly. The agreement is made that Midir may return in one month's time to claim his kiss, a delay that grants Eochaid the time to prepare and perhaps find a way to avert the fulfillment of this unwelcome boon.

When Midir returns, Eochaid's attempts to thwart him prove futile. Midir, invoking his magical prowess, calls upon the powers of the Tuatha Dé Danann, transforming himself and Étaín into swans before the assembled court.

Once transformed, they ascend gracefully into the sky, bound for the Otherworld, leaving the mortal realm and a bewildered court behind. This transformation and departure are symbolic, representing the transcendence of their love from the earthly to the ethereal, and the reclamation of Étaín's divine heritage and her reunion with Midir in the realm of the Tuatha Dé Danann.

Conclusion

As we draw the final pages of "Celtic Mythology: A Collection of the Best Celtic Myths" to a close, we reflect upon a journey that has taken us through the verdant landscapes and tumultuous seas of the Celtic imagination. From the celestial realms of the gods and goddesses to the earth-bound exploits of legendary heroes, we have traversed a world where the lines between the mortal and the divine blur, where magic infuses every rock, tree, and stream, and where the echoes of ancient battles and timeless love stories resound.

We began our odyssey by acquainting ourselves with the divine inhabitants of the Celtic pantheon, delving into the lives and deeds of deities whose powers shape the natural and supernatural worlds. Through these tales, we gleaned insights into the Celtic understanding of the cosmos, where gods and goddesses are not just rulers but participants in the drama of existence, each with their own stories, passions, and vulnerabilities.

Our narrative then shifted to the mortal plane, where figures like Cú Chulainn, Fionn Mac Cumhaill, and Oisín took center stage. Through their epic quests and heroic deeds, we were reminded of the values that define Celtic heroism: courage, loyalty, and a deep connection to the land and its lore. These stories, rich with adventure and wisdom, serve as a testament to the enduring spirit of the Celtic people, their love of storytelling, and their profound understanding of the human condition.

We also embarked on a journey through the diverse branches of Celtic mythology, exploring the unique flavors of Irish, Scottish, Welsh, Breton, Cornish, and Manx traditions. This exploration revealed the rich mosaic of Celtic cultural narratives, each contributing its own voice to the grand chorus of Celtic myth. Through this kaleidoscope of tales, we came to appreciate the diversity and unity of the Celtic heritage, a testament to the adaptability and resilience of these ancient cultures.

The heart of the book was dedicated to the myths themselves, each chosen for its beauty, significance, and ability to captivate the imagination. From the tragic beauty of "The Children of Lir" to the martial valor and tragedy of "The Cattle Raid of Cooley," from the wisdom of "The Salmon of Knowledge" to the eternal love story of "Tristan and Iseult," we were transported into the heart of Celtic mythology, experiencing firsthand the power of these ancient narratives to inspire, educate, and entertain.

I hope you have enjoyed this exploration into the world of Celtic Mythology. If you would like to share your feedback, it is greatly appreciated if you could take a minute to leave us a review on Amazon. It really helps us to continue producing books that readers love!

And finally, if you liked this book, please keep an eye out for the other books in this series, also available for sale on Amazon as well as through many other online retailers. The other books in this series include:

- Roman Mythology: A Collection of the Best Roman Myths
- Norse Mythology: A Collection of the Best Norse Myths
- Egyptian Mythology: A Collection of the Best Egyptian Myths
- Greek Mythology: A Collection of the Best Greek Myths

Printed in Great Britain
by Amazon